AF436178

The Inner Journey of a Traveler

"Who Am I?"

From Fear to Love and Freedom

ARMAND ALTMAN

This edition is published in India
by Arunachala Publication,
Shanti Neelam, 606 604 Adiannamalai, India.

ISBN 979-10-91141-04-8
Printed by Lulu.com in November 2012.

India Library Cataloguing in Publication data available.
Library of Congress Cataloguing in Publication data available.

Table of Contents

Acknowledgments

I am lovingly inspired by my children, family, soulful friends, and especially my friend Tilicho who has been my caring critic and wise editor.

I am committed to donating 50% of all book sales to Shanti Children's Project, a non-profit organization serving impoverished children described more fully in the conclusion.

Dedication

This book is dedicated to the great
Indian Sage Ramana Maharshi who lived in
the sacred mountain of Arunachala.

"The Dance of the Ego,

in this world, if the ego rises,

all else will rise; if it subsides

all else will subside as well."

Ramana Maharshi

My Life Journey From 5 to 77 Years Old

While completing the rough draft of this book, I invited family, friends, spiritual seekers and a few spiritual teachers to review my rough draft, encouraging them to offer any suggestions or perspectives about how they experienced reading the rough draft.

Much to my surprise, I received recommendations to include more of my personal life journey, which would relate to the background of this book. What follows is a Zen like summary of my life story.

Born in 1934, I was the youngest sibling of two older sisters who genuinely loved me, in spite of my being a bit challenging on occasion.

My Father and his second wife had a daughter who was my younger sister. Over the years, and also during challenging times, we were very loving and supportive of each other.

I had a happy and healthy childhood for the first eight years of my life, until I was informed by my parents that I would be sent out of state to a residential military school the following month.

Shocked and unhappy with their decision, I did not understand why this was happening, and I had no influence to change their mind. My three years of military school were very traumatic and significantly impacted how I felt about myself, my parents and all people in authority. As a result of this experience I felt a mixture of love and deep mistrust toward my parents for many years.

As I began to inwardly ask the question "Who am I?", I also began to live in my inner world of fantasy. I felt a deep and special connection with trees and birds flying so freely. Many times when I was feeling sad and alone I would sit beneath a special large oak tree in a field next to the military school, and feel that this was my home.

In addition to trying to manage my personal crisis of being required to attend military school, other children and I were subjected to emotional and physical abuse from a number of teachers, most of whom were emotionally dysfunctional and incompetent. Also, as younger children, we had to protect ourselves from older students who attempted to sexually abuse us.

My parents divorced when I was 10

years old, and between the age of 10 and 17, I lived alternating years in Buffalo, N. Y. and Los Angeles. My mother had moved primarily for her health. I was very unhappy with this intense change in my home life.

Between the ages of 14 and 16, I was expelled from two high schools in Los Angeles because of my poor attendance and my not "conforming to the regulations of the school system". I dropped out of high school in my 12th year and experienced a mixture of happiness and sadness throughout my teenage years.

I joined the Navy during the Korean war in 1951, I was 17 years old. I spent 4 years aboard two ships, one of which was a hospital ship located in South Korea as the medical support for thousands of injured and dying soldiers fighting in the Korean War.

During my 4 years in the Navy I also completed and received a high school equivalency degree. After I was discharged in 1955 at age 21, I had no plans for work or school and had no deep awareness of who I was. The four years in the Navy, along with the two years aboard the hospital ship where I witnessed severely injured and dying men every day, resulted in a minor 'post traumatic stress disorder', which I lived with for 2 to 3 years after my discharge.

During the first year following my discharge I felt confused, occasionally depressed. Working at odd jobs, my most pleasant and significant one was selling Christmas trees for my uncle and cousin in Texas.

On Christmas Eve 1956, I met a homeless man. He asked me if he could warm his hands over the large barrel of burning wood I had been standing by to keep warm. Inviting him to stand with me at the barrel, we had nearly an hour of conversation. I asked him questions about his life, he asked me questions about mine.

By the time he was ready to leave he asked me if I could give him a little money to buy some food. I immediately gave him what I had in my pocket which was 2 dollars.

Walking away from the hot barrel of burning wood, he said quite firmly as he looked directly into my eyes, "Stop wandering around aimlessly, focus your mind on education and going to college".

That night I was unable to sleep, being intensely reflective about the homeless man's advice. Christmas morning I told my uncle and cousin that I was going to California to begin college.

In my initial college years at Los Angeles City Community college I became a competitive gymnast, and in taking a few awakening courses in psychology, philosophy, and politics, I became inspired educationally to continue undergraduate school. At a later time I attended graduate school part and full time for a number of years.

My decision to change my life of aimlessly wandering, since being discharged from the Navy and attending college and graduate school was very significant. I was feeling more positive and empowered as I felt more self respect and more committed to be aware of the nature of my emotional patterns…my ego/mind.

I experienced a variety of inspiring, challenging life experiences during the decades of the 60's, 70's and 80's which were a catalyst in my personal growth and deepening awareness of the spiritual path, and global political and economic dramas and wars which are impacting on the suffering of people throughout the world.

A few of my more significant experiences in the 60's and the 70's were my active protests against the Vietnam War, and my support for the Civil Rights of all minorities, including women. This was also a time period in which I used mind state altering drugs which were spiritually transformative initially, but ultimately were only a temporary awakening.

A significant and inspiring opportunity was becoming an advocate in my work with developmental and psychiatrically disabled children and adults who were, or previously had been institutionalized.

During the time period from the 60's and throughout the years ahead, I was inspired by the philosophies of Buddha, the Tao and Hindu Vedic scriptures of the Upanishads...especially the scriptures of Advaita Vedanta, embraced by many Awakened sages, past and present...which is also attractive to many Quantum physicists inspired to understand the complexities and illusions of the nature of the Universe.

This was also a very awakening and changing time period in my life when I became the father of my son, in my first marriage of three years, and the father of my daughter and son, in my second marriage of thirteen years.

During this very joyful and challenging time period after the 70's and 80's, and many years of feeling happy and peaceful in my second marriage, unexpected changes occurred. My wife and I mutually agreed to end our marriage after 13 years.

Although we continued to be friends, I began to experience brief periods of existential discontent, and a growing sadness about my changing life.

I was aware that I was responsible for much of the stress and conflicts which occurred in my relationships; especially with the two Mothers of my children, and a few other women that I had brief intimate relationships with, over many years.

I soon decided after becoming aware that I was not happy with who I was and my way of living, to let go/resign from my work as an advocate, therapist, and project director. With honest awareness, I was unclear about "who am I ?" at a deeper inner level.

At this time I began to travel to Guatemala, Europe, Middle East countries, China and Tibet, and especially Thailand, Nepal, India and other countries in South East Asia. My deepest interest spiritually was visiting and living part time each year in India.

During my 27 years of travel I had the opportunity to live in India and Nepal for brief time periods, with some very awakened and not awakened Yogis, living in mountains and caves, in small villages and one large city.

One of the most special volunteer opportunities I experienced, which was another awakening moment in my life, was meeting Mother Teresa in Calcutta, India. She served the most severely impoverished and suffering children, adults and families.

I was deeply shocked to actually see and experience how impoverished, and how much suffering human beings are experiencing in their lives each day. I also realize that there are hundreds of millions more who also experience this level of suffering throughout the world.

I assisted as a volunteer, being directly supportive of young and older adults who were dying, who were in need of, as Mother Teresa described (to all volunteers), "genuine love, a sacred and healing energy".

Another unique experience I had which was also special, is visiting and living with the Hunzas, a tribe of people who lived in the high mountains (3,500 meters/10,000 feet) of Pakistan. The Hunzas lived a full and active life, many up to 100 years of age. A number of the older villagers I met were between 100 and 110 years of age. The Hunzas were living in a very beautiful, sacred setting of the K2 mountain ranges with a challenging winter climate, mostly 'off the grid', very limited electricity.

I was in awe to see and experience in two months, how the adults had a calmness and kindness toward each other in how they lived and communicated. The 30 to 40 children were a surprise as I observed them sitting on the ground in their outdoor school (no school rooms); during school they were all very attentive in listening to the teacher, and also while actively playing together after school, I did not observe any anger or aggression toward each other.

Anthropologists discovered the reason for the Hunzas living such a long life, in spite of the challenging winter season, is primarily related to their having very limited stress in their personal lives, and in their relationships, which I also experienced in the two months that I lived in their community.

It is now being discovered in medical and psychological research that "stress" is a significant factor contributing to many human diseases, including cancer, depression, and conflicts in the majority of human relationships.

I now feel that the past forty years of my life has been what I describe as a special "gift". I experienced a number of intense challenges, unexpected but significant awakening lessons, genuine Love and Freedom, and more joyous appreciation of life…especially with my children in the continuing years as we celebrated traveling and other life experiences together.

Foreword

On my personal and spiritual journey over the last twenty eight years, I explored the meaning of life in a much deeper way than I had previously experienced. When I began my travels, I was not at peace or happy with myself. I was genuinely searching for a less stressful, less materialistic life.

Having experienced extraordinary sacred sites and very impoverished living conditions, I encountered great wisdom and ignorance. Gaining Self-knowledge, I began to experience a letting go of ego/mind. It helped to release much stress and unhappiness, while I sought a life of true awakening.

From my experiences in the last 28 years of life transition, and based upon the experience of many credible psychological, social researchers and sages, I came to the conclusion that it is possible to change our life long habits and patterns that we often assume cannot be changed.

When we are truly inspired and genuinely believe we can change one or more of our life habits and patterns, we are able to make one or more significant life changes. Gaining knowledge of the nature of our mind, and the recently discovered "Intelligence of the Heart" (inner wisdom) by spiritually sensitive scientists, can also be supportive of change. The understanding of our True Nature helps in bringing this change and dissolving the ego/mind. There is a letting go of life-long attachments, expectations and fears related to past or future which prevent living in the present.

I am hopeful that you will find the theme of this book supportive of your life journey, including this special quote by a highly respected sage, Ramana Maharshi: "Unless and until a man embarks on this quest of the true Self, doubt and uncertainty will follow his footsteps through life. The greatest kings and statesmen try to rule others when in their hearts of hearts they know that they cannot rule themselves. Yet the greatest power is at the command of the man who has penetrated to his inmost depth...What is the use of knowing about everything else when you do not yet know who you are? Men avoid this enquiry into the true Self, but what else is there so worthy to be undertaken?"

During my years of travel I was inspired through reading and experiencing the profound spiritual teachings offered over the past 3,000 years by a number of enlightened sages, including Ramana Maharshi. In the following excerpt he briefly described his Self-realization experience:

At the age of sixteen and a half, during a visit to his uncle's home, Ramana, unexpectedly had a dying experience, and realized during his imitating the dying experience as he lay on the floor in a rigor mortis position...

"That this body dies but the Spirit that transcends it cannot be touched by death. That means I am the deathless "Spirit". The 'I' was something very real. From that moment on the "I" was the Self. Fear of death had vanished once and for all. Absorption in the Self continued unbroken from that time on. Whether the body was engaged in talking, reading or anything else, I was still centered on "I". Previous to my fear of dying, I had no clear perception of my Self, and was not consciously attracted to it. I felt no direct interest in it, much less any inclination to dwell permanently in it."

Following this realization Ramana left his home, and for the next twenty-five years lived in caves in the sacred mountain of Arunachala, Tiruvannamalai, where he observed almost total silence.

During the last twenty-seven years of his life Ramana lived in an ashram built at the base of Arunachala, where he began to briefly respond to questions from a growing number of visitors and devotees that were spiritually drawn to experience his enlightened presence.

His singular response to the many questions related to finding inner peace was that one should embrace 'Self-enquiry' by asking the question, "Who Am I ?" The first 'I' is the ego. Inquiry about the source of 'I' has the effect of directing the ego 'I' back to the mind, and merging it as its conscious source, the Self, which is also described as Enlightenment.

Ramana advised devotees and spiritual seekers to discover the real source of the ego by exploring within with keen intellect, and by regulating the breath, speech and mind, as one would do to recover an object which has fallen into a deep well.

A quieting of the mind is therefore automatically brought about by paying attention to the breath. Control of your breath means watching with the mind, the flow of breath'.

There will be a brief clarification in the following pages about the meaning and potential spiritual significance of 'Self-

Enquiry'. Hopefully this book, except for a few terms and concepts you may not be familiar with, which will be defined on an appropriate page, is supportive of your continuing life journey.

Chapter 1 - Introduction

Each individual has the potential to realize one's True Self. This Realization occurs when there is Self-knowledge and the dissolution of ego.

As the sage Ramana Maharshi has stated: "All religions begin with the existence of the individual, the world and God. So long as the ego lasts these three will remain separate. To abide, egoless, in the Self, is the true Reality."

It is the mind/ego that prevents us from realizing and truly experiencing our undivided Natural State: Love. The majority of spiritual books and sacred scriptures over the past 3000 years share a similar belief and teach that: **Self-awareness leads to a profound transformation and the realization of our True Nature.**

Love, God, Heart (not your organic heart), Silence, One, That, the Absolute are all synonyms of Self. All religions point at the same eternal reality using different words. However, and regrettably, violence and war among some religions have prevented the Realization of true Love and Peace. **Yet, silence through prayer or meditation is highly recommended by all religions and great**

Sages. This is the timeless place where Love and Freedom abide.

Prayers, or meditation, are supportive in connecting and eventually merging with the True Self. They assist individuals in quieting their mind and in becoming more aware of their re-occurring mind tapes.

I use the term mind tapes (which is ego) to describe re-occurring streams of thought; desire, fantasies, fears, etc., which all human beings experience. Mind tapes often related to past and future, contribute to one's continuing stress and unhappiness.

We all have the potential to detach from mind tapes and eventually realize the Self by practicing Self-enquiry. Awareness allows one to let go of expectations, attachments and delusions of being the doer. This concept of the 'doer' as the ego/mind prevents Self-Realization as Advaita Vedanta Vedanta scriptures have stated.

Yet in reality, the majority of people including myself, may at times be exclusively identified as a doer, a student, a spiritual seeker, a parent, a worker...and may not be aware of the undivided Self. This identification as a doer results in believing in the ego/mind with many expectations and attachments.

The challenge is to be aware and live and work in the reality of the world we are experiencing without being a doer. To be truly inspired we need to let go and not be attached to our ego/mind and expectations, and maintain a focus on the present moment.

Being aware in the present moment is Self-Realization. Although the Self is who you truly are, It needs to be realized. Self-enquiry, "Who am I?", leads to this realization by finding the Source of everything, the real I: Consciousness. By being conscious, ego automatically dissolves as darkness under the light. This is why Consciousness, the True Self, also means Love or Freedom.

Chapter 2

Perspectives and Being Conditioned

In my travels I met and experienced many credible and not so credible spiritual teachers in a variety of different settings throughout the world, such as in caves, mountain tops, secluded forests, temples, ashrams, and in large cities.

An unexpected life event occurred six years ago after returning from India during the time I was visiting my children in Vermont.

One morning, while on the phone with my daughter, I began to experience numbness in my face and on my left arm. When I described what I was feeling, her immediate response was, "Dad you may be experiencing a stroke, go immediately to the hospital emergency room. I'll meet you there in the next hour!"

In the short taxi ride to the hospital, I experienced a growing fear and sadness that I might die in the next hour and not have the opportunity to see my daughter and my two sons to let them know how much I love them.

At the emergency admittance office I was immediately sent to the medical treatment room. While being 'hooked up' and given intravenous preventative care for what was then confirmed as a neurological stroke, I began to experience an unexpected 'letting go', a feeling that I was not my body and mind/ego.

I was very fortunate to have had only a minor stroke, much to the doctor's surprise. The stroke experience awakened me to the reality of a deepening inner peace with a clear awareness. For the rest of my recovery, and through the following months and years, the clarity has remained that there is only the present moment. The momentary fear I had about dying in the taxi and the first few hours in the hospital had simply dissolved.

What I described as my ego/mind does on occasion arise, however, much less often now as I spent time with my family, friends, and continued to travel. I experience more joy and inner peace, living in the present moment, with few expectations and attachments.

For a variety of understandable reasons which are discussed in this book, the majority of spiritual seekers and devotees during part or throughout their lives feel unable to truly experience their Natural State. Most often, this is because of fear and emotional insecurity experienced throughout childhood and unexpected traumatic life experiences.

They may experience periods of deep awakening, but these experiences often diminish as ego/mind becomes attracted and attached to past traditional styles of living, which previously created stress and unhappiness in their lives.

I believe it is possible, if you are deeply moved in your life as a growing number of spiritual seekers and others are, to realize the Self through the continued practice of Self-inquiry.

The surrendering of the ego is the challenge I have been experiencing for many years. I continue to practice living in the present moment as much as possible. I try to be aware and let go of whatever attachments may arise that creates stress and keeps me attached and controlled by my ego/mind.

There are many different spiritual paths, more or less direct. They all eventually become one upon reaching the peak. The search for liberation and happiness is the common base. Yet, the reality is that a majority of people simply live their life without searching for this liberation and without being aware of who they really are.

When genuine Awakening occurs, it is the beginning of a deepening process of dissolving expectations, attachments and concerns about past and future. By being aware, no longer are we controlled by our ego/mind (the ongoing thought/fantasy patterns), the source of our agitation, sadness, loneliness, anger and suffering.

Historically written credible sacred scriptures, enlightened sages, and our personal insights and experiences teach that the ego is the primary source and catalyst for re-occurring mind tapes (thoughts and fantasies). These tapes, without awareness, block the realization of true Self.

It is in a spiritually existential moment, when we truly become aware of our ego mind tapes that a spiritual and emotional transformation occurs! We then begin consciously living in the present, not the past or the future. We begin to let go of the expectations and attachments of being the doer.

It is apparent by most evidence that we are continually influenced and controlled by our ego. We need to make continued efforts to dissolve the ego through the use of a creative visualization process that will be described in the forthcoming pages.

You will become more aware and inspired by remaining committed to your spiritual search and life journey. Your relationships and work will more easily change in spite of questioning or judgments by family, friends or traditional society. Serious depression and life threatening illness will be avoided.

As you continue your spiritual journey, you will be meeting a few genuinely awakened teachers, (and some who are not genuinely awakened), gaining new knowledge and sharing with other travelers and spiritual seekers.

You will be guided by your heightened awareness, inner wisdom, experiencing new levels of silence. Your ego/mind, which you soon realize is an illusion cloaked in the thought forms of mind and fantasies, has less control over you.

Some aspects of your personality and energy will change. You may be motivated to continue traveling or return to your home-base or possibly create a new home-base to experience life more simply, more deeply, consciously and joyously.

You may not be as affected emotionally by the social and political regional and world dramas, including violence and economic instabilities occurring locally and throughout the world.

My perspective of following the visualization practice will support you to experience a renewed or continuing personal inner peace.

This practice has been very helpful for me and many others who have used this process. You may begin to feel more inner peace as you become more aware, and committed to understanding the nature of your mind and your life patterns.

It is your mind that has the potential to change and transform through silence. The ego's mind tapes of the past and future are similar to the addictions that the majority of people have who are attached to one or more recreational and legal drugs, sugar products, money, power, etc.

Your ego is a controlling and negative energy that impacts upon and influences your relationship with yourself, family, friends and intimate partners, as we all have experienced in our lives at different times.

Your ego also impacts upon your work, especially in the way of communicating personal feelings, concerns, and responding or reacting to the communications and possible judgments of others.

It is self-evident in our life experiences, and throughout the history of genuine spiritual seekers, and past/present enlightened sages that if one truly knows oneself, there is a surrender of the ego and ultimately Self-realization, not intellectually, but in everyday life. Intellectual knowledge is not enough as long as one cannot truly believe that *Love, another word for the Self or Consciousness*, is one's True Nature.

A successful process for stopping the mind tapes and helping to believe one's True Nature is Love, is to *visualize* at the moment of the mind tape rising, a positive inner thought or mantra like: "I am love", "I am silence" or other words like "Om", "silence", "love", or any one or more of these words or mantras that feels workable for you.

This creative process has been very helpful for numerous people over many years, and is most effective as a continuing daily silent practice, especially when the ego/mind tape begins to rise and play in your mind.

Over time, change occurs and awareness becomes a daily life reality. You begin to experience a diminishing of your ego and live in the present moment with fewer attachments. This letting go of expectations and fears brings happiness and peace in your everyday life.

Chapter 3

Ramana Maharshi's Responses

Two re-occurring questions raised by visitors and devotees of Ramana Maharshi were:

How does Self Enquiry "Who Am I ?" help me realize the Self? And, how can I let go of my ego and experience Liberation?

The following samples of Ramana Maharshi's responses to these questions may be found clarifying and inspiring:

"By the enquiry "Who am I ?", the thought " Who am I ?" will destroy all other thoughts eventually. And like the stick used for stirring burning pyre, it will itself in the end get destroyed. Then there will arise Self-realization." "Liberation is inquiring into the nature of one's self that is in bondage, and realizing one's True Nature is Liberation."

"The fruit of 'Self-Enquiry' is the realization that the Self is all, and that nothing else is there. If one surrenders one's ego, one realizes the Self...one's natural inherent state."

Chapter 4 - Conclusion.

During my traveling over the past 28 years, I experienced a deepening awareness that true Love and Freedom is our Natural State, as I let go of ego and living in the past and future. This awareness and challenging life moments have offered what I describe as timeless unexpected life lessons.

I am also aware that I will continue to experience happiness and inner peace as well as unexpected challenges, living in the reality of an expanding world. The majority of the world population has been led to believe in, and support the illusion that materialism is a primary value to bring happiness and success. I realized through my spiritual journey that True Happiness, Love and Freedom first have to be found within ourselves.

I complete this book with my personal poem, inspired by a soulful friend:

No matter where I go

here I am

alone and One

always That

home is in my Heart

celebration and Silence

in this moment

Timeless

May you always abide in your heart as:
Existence, Consciousness and Bliss.
Jai Sat Chit Ananda

Shanti Children's Project

Shanti Educational and Support Services where I served as a volunteer during the past 12 years, is a certified non-profit project in Tiruvannamalai, India. The Shanti project is deeply committed to offering financial and emotional support for assisting children age 5 and older whose families (often single parents) are financially very poor, (earning less than $50 American dollars per month). Families cannot afford to have their children attend the public governmental school system because of specific financial costs.

The Indian government which has no tuition costs up to 6th grade, requires all children to pay for their uniforms, and writing materials, which very poor families cannot afford.

Shanti also offers educational financial support beyond 5th grade, and tutoring support every day at the end of the school day, including creative recreational programs and preventative health care, as well as emergency health services for the children. There are more girls than boys in the project because girls are not offered an equal opportunity, to initially begin or complete school beyond the 5th grade, compared to boys throughout India.

I hope this book will contribute to support Shanti's inspiring project.

Contact:

www.shantichildrenproject.org
shantichildrenproject@gmail.com

My e-mail address is: ahaarmand@gmail.com